SWASTICK BOOK BOX
MASON OF WINNERS

SBB

English WRITING BOOK Small Letters

Awesome English Writing Practice Book for Kids

By: **Preeti Garg**

Follow the patterns with your pencil.

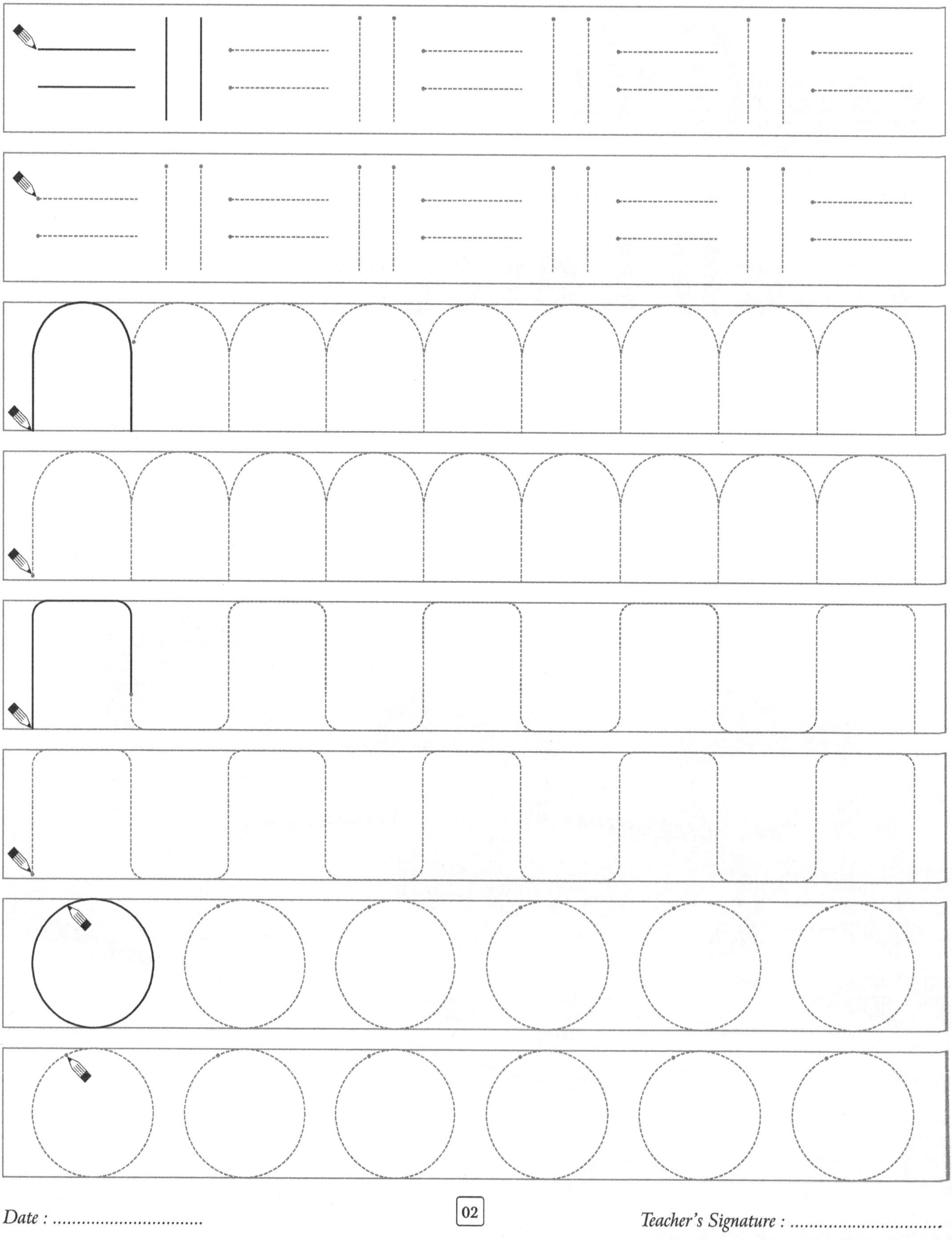

Date : .... Teacher's Signature : ....

Follow the patterns with your pencil.

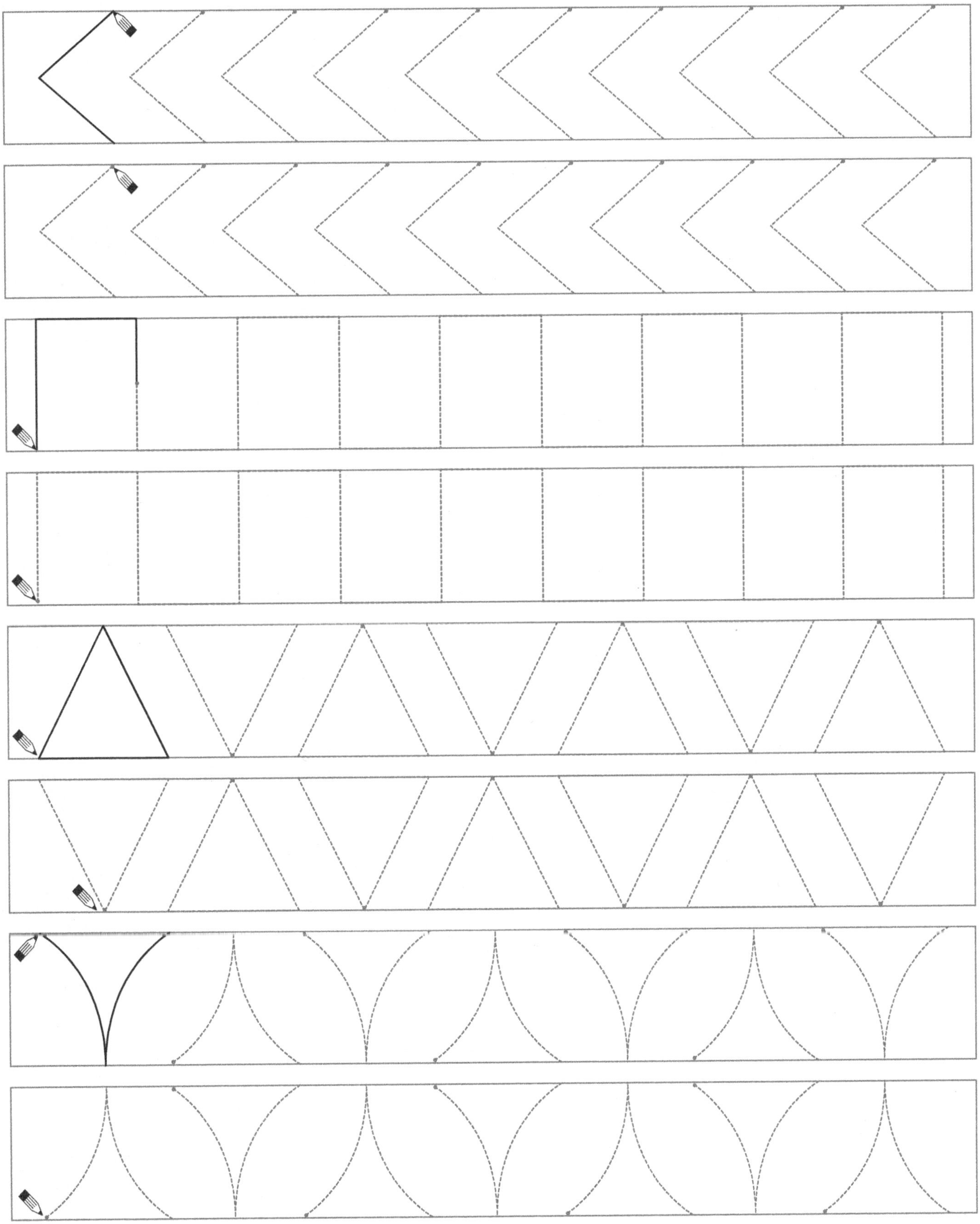

Date : ....

Teacher's Signature : ....

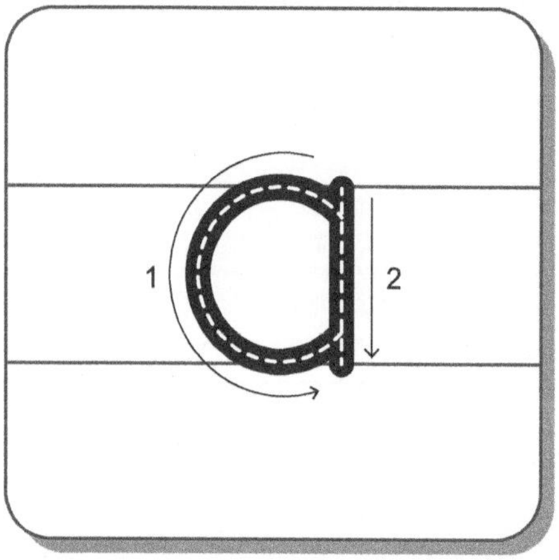

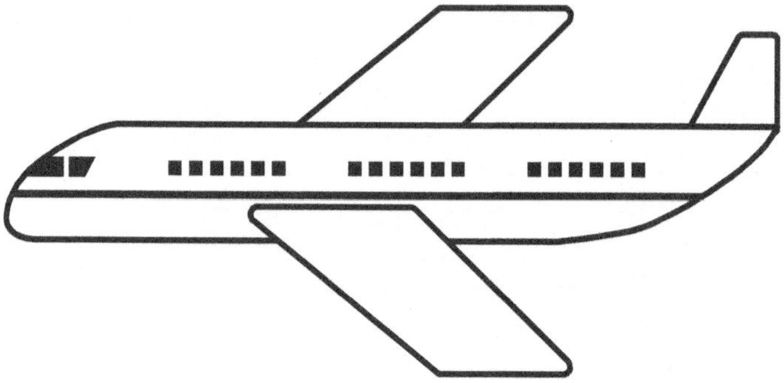

aeroplane

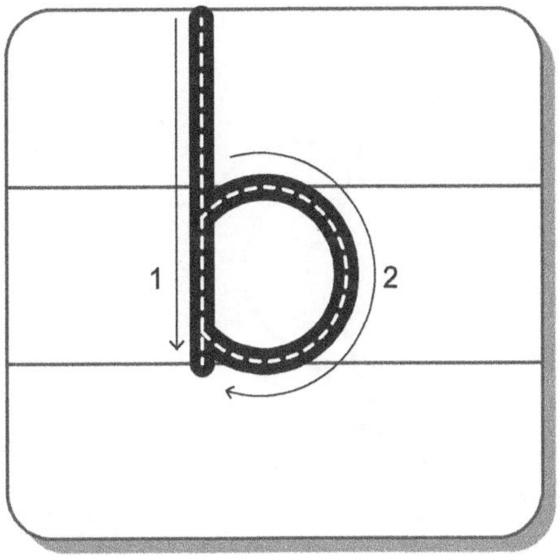

balloons

Date : ....

Teacher's Signature : ....

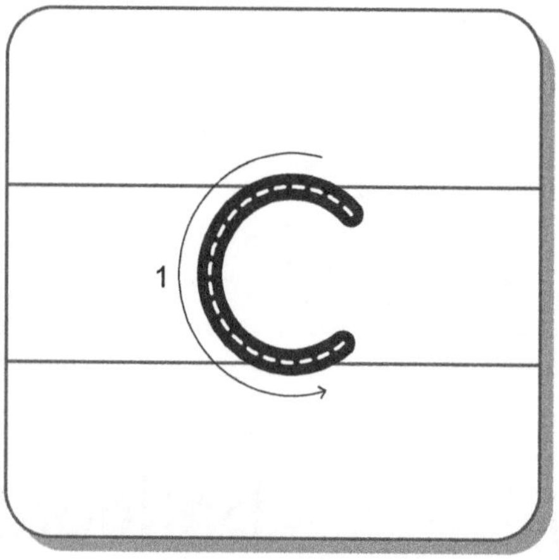

cup

c c c c c c c

c c c c c c c

c c c c c c c

c c c c c c c

c c c c c c c

c c c c c c c

c c c c c c c

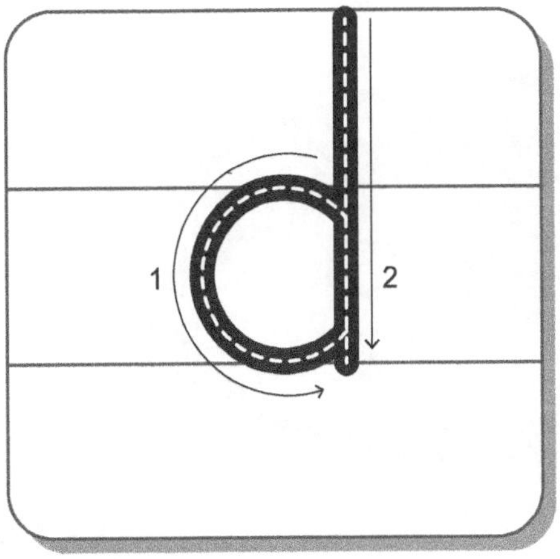

doll

Date : ....

Teacher's Signature : ....

eye

e

Date : ....

Teacher's Signature : ....

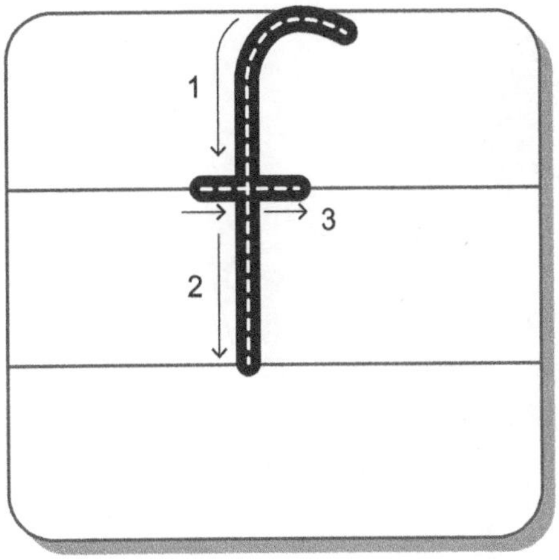

fish

f

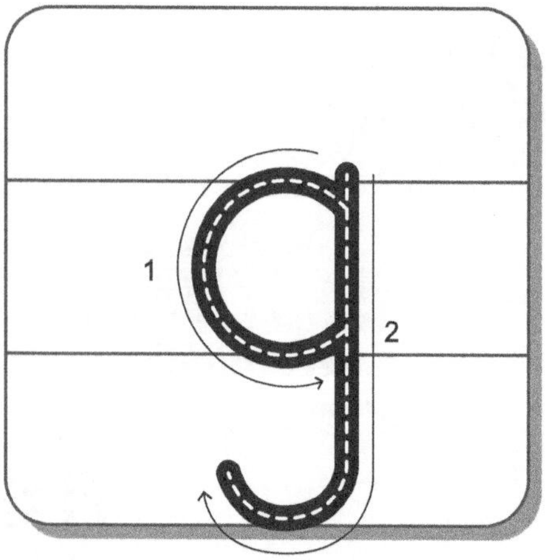

gift

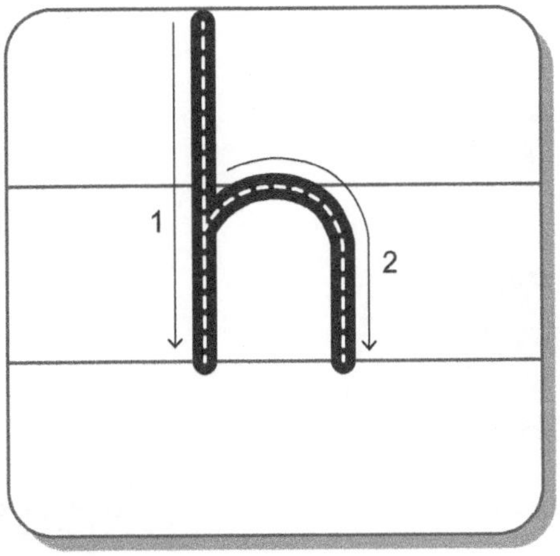

hat

Date : ....

Teacher's Signature : ....

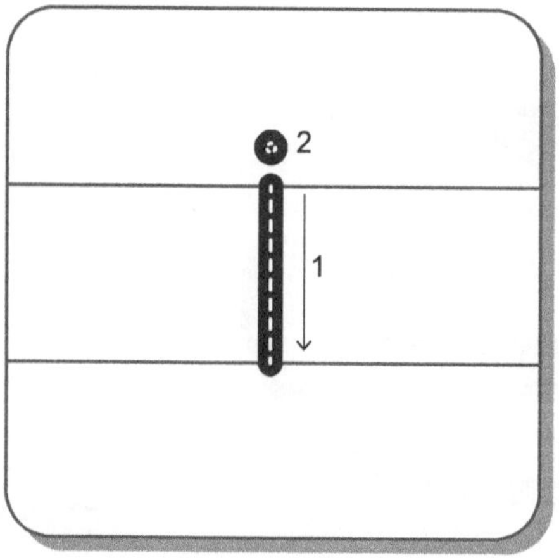

inkpot

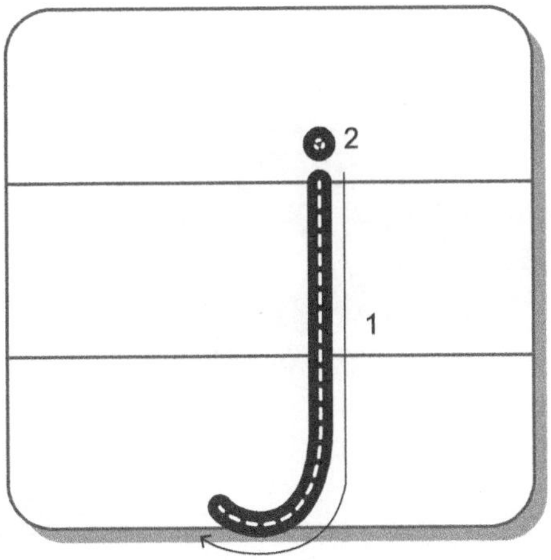

joker

Date : ....

Teacher's Signature : ....

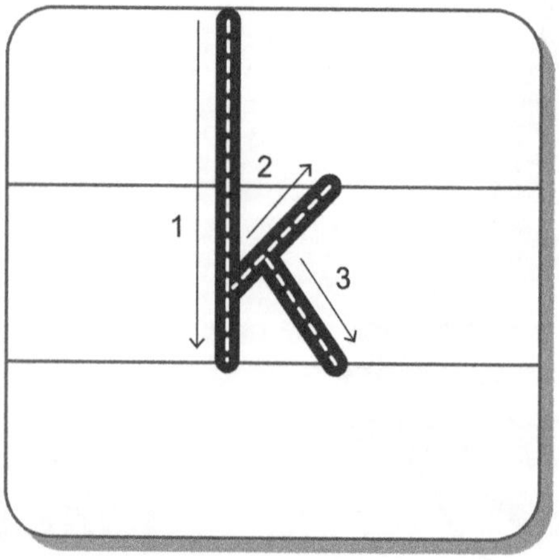

key

k	k	k	k	k	k	k
k	k	k	k	k	k	k
k	k	k	k	k	k	k
k	k	k	k	k	k	k
k	k	k	k	k	k	k
k	k	k	k	k	k	k
k	k	k	k	k	k	k

Date : ....

Teacher's Signature : ....

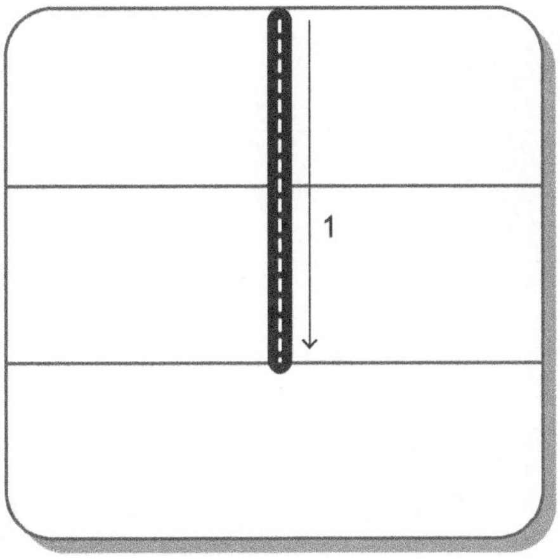

lips

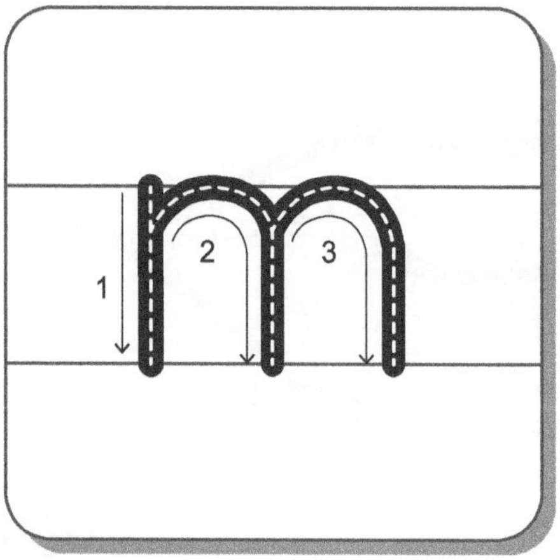

monkey

m	m	m	m	m	m	m
m	m	m	m	m	m	m
m	m	m	m	m	m	m
m	m	m	m	m	m	m
m	m	m	m	m	m	m
m	m	m	m	m	m	m
m	m	m	m	m	m	m

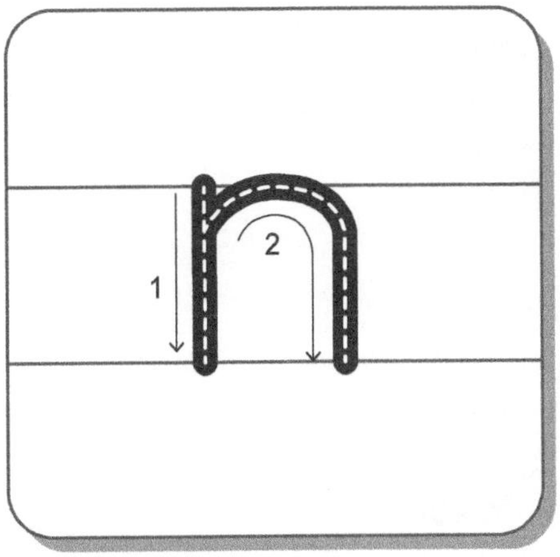

nest

n	n	n	n	n	n	n
n	n	n	n	n	n	n
n	n	n	n	n	n	n
n	n	n	n	n	n	n
n	n	n	n	n	n	n
n	n	n	n	n	n	n
n	n	n	n	n	n	n

Date : .... *Teacher's Signature :* ....

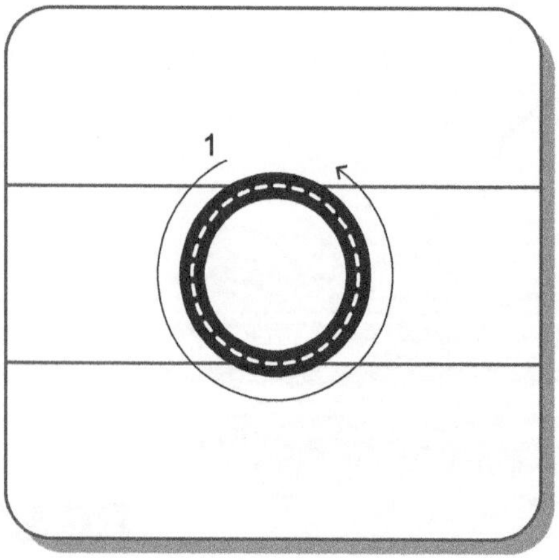

owl

Date : ....

Teacher's Signature : ....

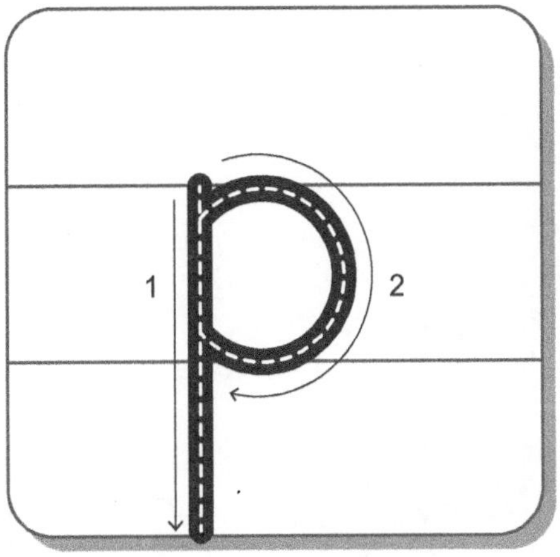

parrot

Date : ....

Teacher's Signature : ....

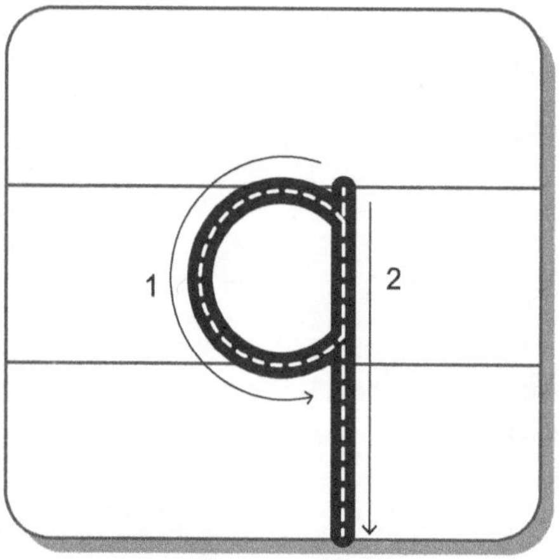

queen

q

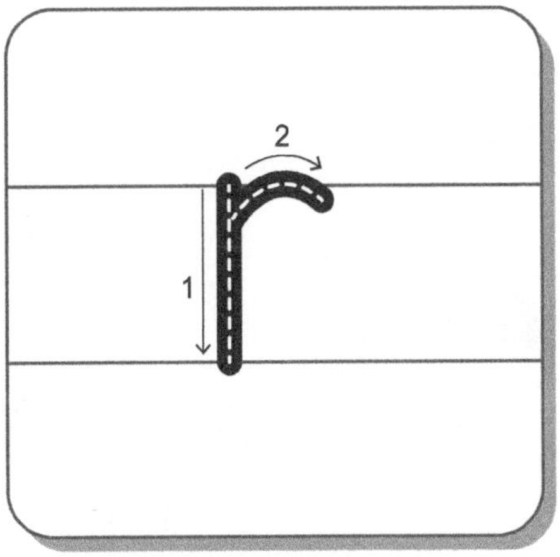

rat

r

Date : ....

Teacher's Signature : ....

snake

s	s	s	s	s	s	s
s	s	s	s	s	s	s
s	s	s	s	s	s	s
s	s	s	s	s	s	s
s	s	s	s	s	s	s
s	s	s	s	s	s	s
s	s	s	s	s	s	s

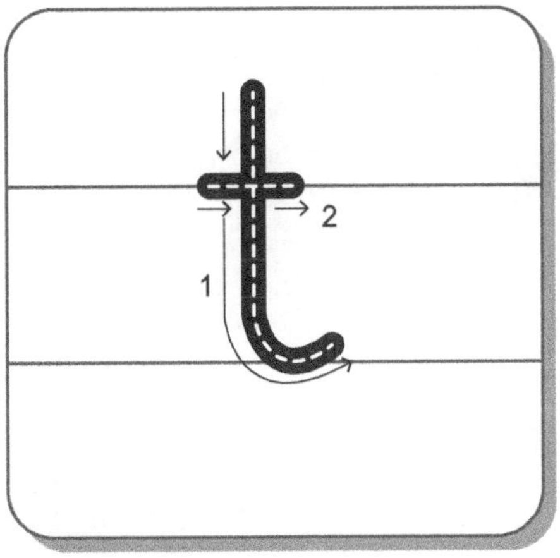

tomato

t

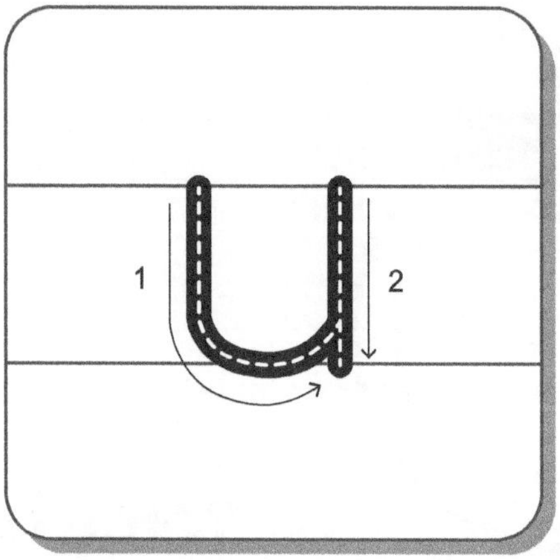

umbrella

Date : ....

Teacher's Signature : ....

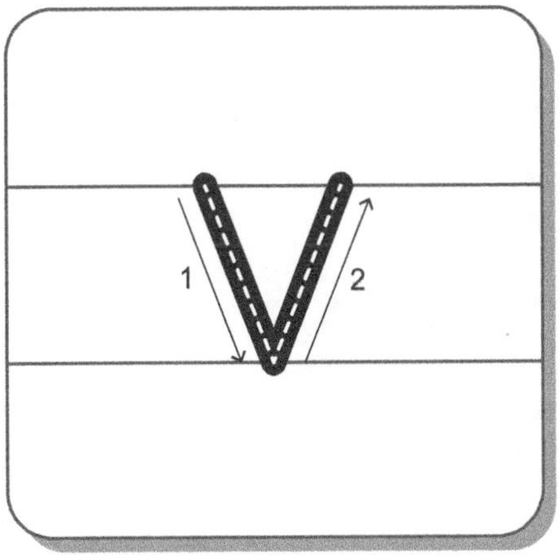

violin

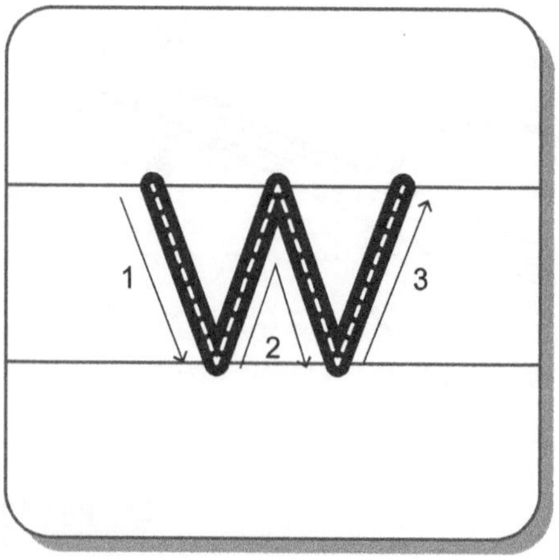

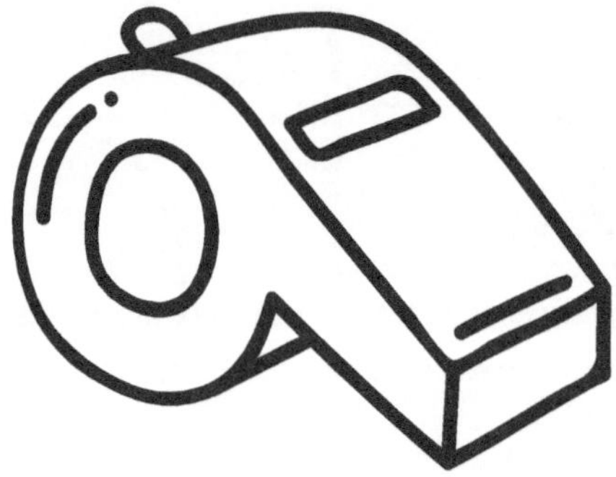

whistle

w

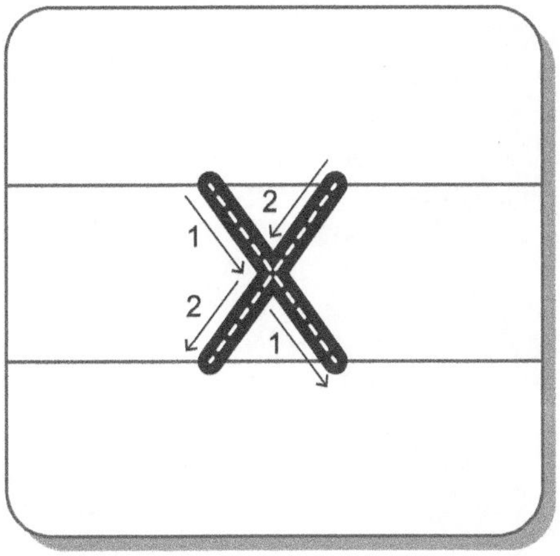

x-mas tree

Date : ....

Teacher's Signature : ....

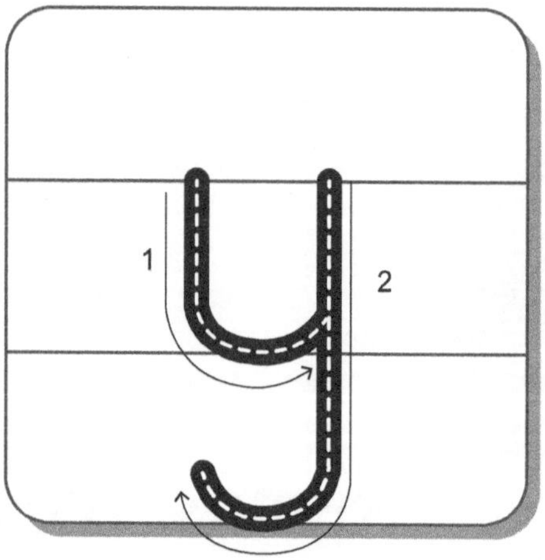

yak

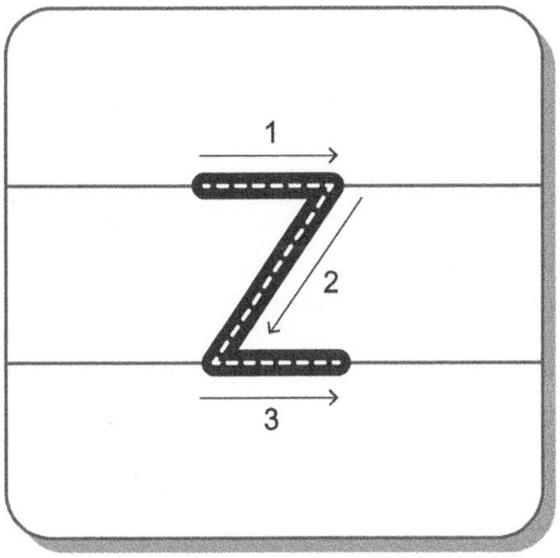

zebra

Date : ....

Teacher's Signature : ....

Say and trace the letters.

a	b	c	d	e	f
g	h	i	j	k	l
m	n	o	p	q	r
s	t	u	v	w	x
y	z				

Write the letters a to z.

Date : ....

Teacher's Signature : ....

Write the missing letters from a to z.

a	b	c		e	f
g			j	k	
m	n		p		r
	t	u		w	
	z				

Write the letter that comes after the given letter.

n		w		u	
k		o		d	

Write the letter that comes before the given letter.

	y		t		j
	r		i		c

Date : ....

Teacher's Signature : ....

Match and write the letters with objects they start with.

b

l

q

v

c

s

g

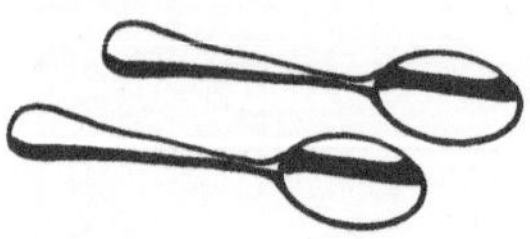

n

Date : ....

Teacher's Signature : ....